THE RAW TRUTH

Entrepreneurship Cooked Right!

By John D. Monjazi

Copyright © 2014 **John D. Monjazi**
All rights reserved.

ISBN: 1499271700
ISBN 13: **978-1499271706**

Contents

Preface: I'm Not Here to Waste Your Time!

Get Entrepreneurship Right
What Is an Entrepreneur?
Exercise One: Entrepreneurial Traits
Exercise Two: Are You an Entrepreneurial Person?

First Miracle: The Entrepreneurial Idea
Identify the Idea
Exercise Three: Prepare for the Miracle
Exercise Four: Put Your Idea to Paper
Develop the Idea

Second Miracle: The Team
Steps to Building a Team

Exercise Five: Weed Out Negative Influences
Prep for the Team
When to Look for a Partner
Attract and Retain Talent

Third Miracle: Window of Opportunity
The Miracle Explained
Timing

Fourth Miracle: Live or Die
Respect the Success
Be Honest: Recognize Epic Failures

Doesn't End Here

Preface

I'm Not Here to Waste Your Time!

This book is raw ("to the point")—short and simple. I designed it to show you the raw truth about entrepreneurship and how it goes hand in hand with reaching your personal expectation of success. Like most of you, I am sick and tired of authors who use gimmicks like, "Guaranteed to make you successful," or "I'll make you a millionaire."

First, thanks for picking up this book. You made a great choice. Second, nothing in life is a guarantee (except death). Third, as an entrepreneurial person myself, I wrote this book to show you the truth about the entrepreneurial lifestyle.

How does this book do that? In the next chapter, I give you the real-world definition of "entrepreneurship." By the end of that chapter, you will know, without a doubt, if you are or want to be an entrepreneurial person. Then, I'll show you the four miracles required to reach success as an entrepreneur. There is a reason I call them "miracles": you can't buy them, you can't ask for them, you can work tirelessly for them, and even then you might not receive them. Last but not least, I'll show you the biggest problem you and I both suffer from—waiting.

What This Book Is Not

I'm not here to help you save money in your next venture. I'm not here to tell you things you already know; there are a million books at your disposal that can do that for you. I'm here to give you the raw truth about entrepreneurship.

This book is not "I'll tell you about my story of success." It is a "You tell me if you want to ~~be~~ *struggle to be* successful" book. You are your best supporter and worst enemy!

This book is designed for you to make it your own. It's time to take control of your current and future circumstances. Enjoy.

> You can't connect the dots looking forward; you can only connect them looking backwards. So you have to trust that the dots will somehow connect in your future. You have to trust in something—your gut, destiny, life, karma, whatever. This approach has never let me down, and it has made all the difference in my life.
>
> —Steve Jobs

Get Entrepreneurship Right

As I began to write this book, I looked out my window and saw a hawk about twenty-five feet away from me. I looked at it and said, "Wow, what a beautiful creature." As I watched the hawk soaring gracefully through the sky, two large crows bombed in out of seemingly nowhere and nearly crashed into the hawk. As the crows dove repeatedly and violently close to the hawk's head, they hollered out *ca-caw*! The hawk stood its ground as if nothing happened. I'm not sure what type of a hawk it was, but the crows were much larger. Within a few seconds, more crows began to appear. Instead of two crows trying to attack the hawk, it turned into three, then four. The hawk would just duck its head as the crows bombed down on it. After a few minutes the hawk successfully flew away, and the crows retreated.

The hawk is a perfect representation of an entrepreneurial person, someone who knows who they are, inside and out. The hawk knew, without a doubt, its position in the food chain and was not bothered at all by the chaos that is life. Entrepreneurial people don't fight life, they fight for it.

What is an Entrepreneur?

Many people have heard the term "entrepreneur," but the sad truth is most people have no idea what it means. However, I have come to realize that when we identify ourselves as "entrepreneurs," it is our own fault so many people then do not know what the word "entrepreneur" means.

I was just as guilty as anyone. When people would ask me what I do for work, I used to say, "I'm an entrepreneur," hoping they would say, "Wow, that's awesome!" More often than not they would ask me, "Wait, so what do you do?" Then I would have to explain how I wear multiple hats—making sales calls, hiring employees, managing projects, reviewing legal documents, hosting meetings, managing finances, etc. If I would have told them, "I run a tech start-up that builds iOS and Android applications for local restaurants," then they may have said, "Wow, that's cool!" Why? Because it actually answers their question. Being an entrepreneur is not an occupation!

> **Comment [1]:** Good paragraph and good ending to complete the thought.

The word "entrepreneur" is most effectively used to describe a mind-set. My definition of the word "entrepreneur" is: a functioning person who is mildly gifted with schizophrenia, paranoia, risk aversion, ADD, ADHD, narcissism, and bipolar "disorder," who still has the ability to focus momentarily and get things done. There you have it. Like the rest of this book, I don't sugarcoat any of it. I'll give it to you raw, and it's up to you to cook it for yourself.

Even industry experts, longtime professors of entrepreneurship, and business philosophers wrestle with the basic question, "Are entrepreneurs born or made?" To answer that question, I am going to ask you a set of questions: Can a fish climb a tree quicker than a bear? Can a bear swim faster than a fish? We all possess entrepreneurial traits. Unfortunately, the majority of us are like the fish trying to climb the tree! The message here is to do what you were designed to do, not what you think you should be doing. For example, if you hate sales, get out and do something you love to do—*not* sales. If you don't know what you love to do, then figure it out!

Even though we all possess entrepreneurial traits, some of us have more of those traits than others. For those of you who do not possess many entrepreneurial traits but wish to organize or operate your own business, read on!

Quick story. Tom, the owner of a circus, had two elephants (a female and a male), who produced a baby elephant named Sammy. Sammy was a very curious and high-energy elephant who loved to explore. As Tom began to train Sammy, he noticed how hard it was for Sammy to pay attention to his commands. Tom went into his tool box and grabbed one of the big tent nails and some rope. Tom drilled the nail deep into the ground and tied Sammy to it. Sammy did his best to pull away from the nail, but even at five hundred pounds, he was unable. As time passed, Tom trained Sammy to listen to his commands, but the most interesting part was that Tom no longer needed to tie Sammy to the big nail. Tom would use a normal nail, which a nine-year-old child could pull out, but Sammy did not even try because he believed it was the same nail as the one used when he was a baby. Most of you have likely heard a variation of this story.

The point of this story is that you need to take a close personal inventory of your beliefs about yourself and your capabilities. The "Sammy" scenario happens to all of us, whether we know it or not. Are you willing to try to pull the nail out of the ground for the millionth time and truly believe you can pull it? Do you have the motivation to overcome your current life situation, or are you too beaten down to believe you can take control of your own life?

If you are willing to try, then let's do it together.

First, the number one thing that identifies people as entrepreneurial is they genuinely want to help others solve a problem, whether it's by getting their nails done more quickly or developing a cure for cancer. They see the world as one big bag of problems, and it's their job to drop themselves into the middle of the chaos to make a difference. Many people call them "heroes," "pioneers," "visionaries," or "inventors." I call them "you and me." *We* are the entrepreneurial people.

Second, we think we can do things better than others, from building a rocket that can land itself after delivering a satellite into space (Grasshopper, SpaceX) to creating an armband that can hold your iPhone.

Third, once we find something we believe in, good luck trying to change our minds. We have a terrible habit of focusing on something and forgetting everything else.

Finally, real entrepreneurial people get things done; they don't just talk about their ideas, they make them reality. I'm not saying they go from zero to sixty miles per hour in three seconds; what I mean is they test their product or service with real customers.

    Let's be raw. Some of you have been shaped to believe you don't possess any of the above qualities. It's hard to fight the majority, the complacent, and the average. The truth is that you can be different. You are different. Below, we will find out how different you are. I put together my own litmus test to discover the entrepreneurial traits in you. When answering the questions, be honest with yourself. Let's see where you are.

Your time is limited, so don't waste it living someone else's life. Don't be trapped by dogma—which is living with the results of other people's thinking. Don't let the noise of others' opinions drown out your own inner voice. And most important, have the courage to follow your heart and intuition. They somehow already know what you truly want to become. Everything else is secondary.

—Steve Jobs

Exercise One: Entrepreneurial Traits

Circle YES or NO.

1. Do you feel like you can do anything?
YES / NO

2. Does your current job allow you to help or be of service to another human?

YES / NO

3. Are there people helping you pursue your dream job?

YES / NO

4. Do you love your current job?

YES / NO

5. Are you using your talents at work?

YES / NO

If you circled "no" for most of these questions, you're not alone; most people are in this same position. It is not easy having your dream job. It's not easy even knowing what that might be, or, if you do know, it might not be easy pursuing it. It's time to change your current course, time to wake up the entrepreneurial spirit inside of you!

At eighteen, I worked at Costco for the summer. It was my first robotic job (more commonly known as a "nine to five"), and it was terrible for me. Just to be clear, I am not talking down to people who have robotic jobs, but the truth is you need to get out of those jobs. One day a robot will replace you!

> Your time is limited, so don't waste it living someone else's life. Don't be trapped by dogma—which is living with the results of other people's thinking. Don't let the noise of others' opinions drown out your own inner voice. And most important, have the courage to follow your heart and intuition. They somehow already know what you truly want to become. Everything else is secondary.
>
> —Steve Jobs

Comment [2]: This quote is identical to the one inserted just a few pages above. I think this one fits well with the theme of the preceding text, but the one above works as a connecting piece between sections.

Exercise Two: Are You an Entrepreneurial Person?

Circle YES or NO.

1. Do you hate the way the world works?
YES / NO

2. Do you frequently tell yourself "I can do that or something better"?

YES / NO

3. Do you like being risky (like speeding on the freeway)? Are you comfortable with risk (for example, with your investments, life decisions, etc.)?

YES / NO

4. Do you like improving the way things work for you?

YES / NO

5. Do you listen to your gut to make decisions (not about eating)?

YES / NO

6. Last question, to be answered by someone you trust. Read my definition of an entrepreneur* to a person you trust, and then ask that person, "Do you think I'm an entrepreneur?"

YES / NO

*The word "entrepreneur" is most effectively used to describe a mind-set. My definition of the word "entrepreneur" is: a functioning person gifted with all forms of schizophrenia, paranoia, risk aversion, ADD, ADHD, narcissism, and bipolar

> **Comprehensive Copy..., 4/30/14 3:15 PM**
> **Comment [3]:** This definition could go in a footnote. The footnote could either repeat the entire definition or just provide the reader with the page number where you already defined the word.

"disorder," who still has the ability to focus momentarily and get things done.

If you didn't circle "yes" for every one of the above questions, you really need to wake up the entrepreneurial spirit that I know you have inside yourself. For those of you who answered "yes" for all the above questions, like me, then you are most definitely an entrepreneurial person.

Those of us who live the entrepreneurial lifestyle know it's not an easy one. It's not easy getting made fun of and being told your idea will never work and, most commonly, "You're crazy!" It's not easy telling your wife or husband, "I need to take six months off to pursue my dream." It's not easy telling your parents, "I am going to leave school for a year to see if I can make it as a comedian." (Dave Chappell did just that.) As entrepreneurial people, we have to make it work. Or we die inside.

For those of you who have died, it's time to resurrect yourself. Don't be reckless; we all have our reason why we didn't pursue our dream, but take this time to reevaluate your current situation.

> Here's to the crazy ones—the misfits, the rebels, the troublemakers, the round pegs in the square holes. The ones who see things differently—they're not fond of rules. You can quote them, disagree with them, glorify or vilify them, but the only thing you can't do is ignore them because they change things. They push the human race forward, and while some may see them as the crazy ones, we see genius, because the ones who are crazy enough to think that they can change the world are the ones who do.
>
> —Steve Jobs

Comment [4]: This quote comes from a poster for Apple, and wasn't written by Steve Jobs (based on http://en.wikipedia.org/wiki/Think_different#Text).

Give yourself five minutes to write down

why you didn't pursue your dream:

_____

_____

_____

_____

_____

_____

_____

_____

_____

Read over what you wrote and ask yourself, was it worth it? I'm not here to make you feel guilty. I'm here to show you that the reason you gave for shelving your dream was probably not good enough. Loving parents, wife, kids, etc., will support you if you convince them you truly are ready to follow your dreams. It's time to show them your entrepreneurial side, and it's time to show them your vision. Whether you're female or male, rich or poor, it's time to take the necessary steps to reach the vision you

> **Comment [5]:** Since you say the same thing a few lines later, it seemed redundant to have this idea in there twice.

have always wanted for yourself and your family.

Now that you have a better understanding of what it means to be an "entrepreneur," please do me (and the world) a favor and share this new definition with your friends and family. Waking up the entrepreneurial person inside is just the beginning. The rest of this book focuses on how entrepreneurs reach success.

> Almost everything—all external expectations, all pride, all fear of embarrassment or failure—these things just fall away in the face of death, leaving only what is truly important. Remembering that you are going to die is the best way I know to avoid the trap of thinking you have something to lose. You are already naked. There is no reason not to follow your heart.
>
> —Steve Jobs

First Miracle: The Entrepreneurial Idea

Once I transitioned from learning and started thinking, I finally began to see the big picture. It all started one Friday evening. I had just completed preparing for a presentation. I decided to put my feet up on my desk and lean back in my chair. In my chair, I began to stare at my wall and I realized something.

On my wall, I have inspiring reminders of almost all the different ventures I have joined, co-founded, and created. I don't know why I never noticed it before but for the first time, in a sober way, I was able to simultaneously look at all the things I had done as well as what made them a failure or a success. I quickly grabbed a pen and began to write down the main issues. As I wrote them down, they all fell into four categories. The categories were: the wrong idea (completely my fault); the wrong teammates (also my fault); missed opportunities (still my fault); and, finally, no market adoption (finally, not my fault).

I'm actually as proud of the things we haven't done as the things I have done. Innovation is saying "no" to a thousand things.

—Steve Jobs, May 1997

> **Comment [6]:** Why does this quote have a date but some do not?

Identify the Idea

Welcome to the 4 Miracles, the first of which is the workable idea. Everyone has ideas, but entrepreneurs have ideas that actually solve real-world problems. As an entrepreneurial person, I can assure you it's important and healthy to be having ideas on a consistent basis. However, like the Steve Jobs quote I refer to, what helps us reach success is choosing the right idea by saying no to all the others.

In this first miracle is the idea—not just any idea, but the idea that was specifically meant for you. You know this to be true when you can see the idea from the "end-game" perspective all the way back to your current moment. This is made possible due to your experiences, skills, and talents.

Exercise Three: Prepare for the Miracle

If you have received this miracle or want to receive it, then prepare for it by asking yourself these questions:

1. Do I believe I have a gift, talent, and/or skill that I can offer the world?

2. Am I ready to sacrifice it all for my dream?

3. Can I give myself the time, effort, and financial support (or find it) to pursue my dream?

4 Am I ready to start my own path and take control of my life?

5. Do I have the courage to tell my family and friends about the crazy idea I have and want to pursue?

Tell yourself, "My idea is possible if I make it possible. I will face challenges, adversities, disappointments, but I will prevail; I will make a difference." The first step to preparing to accept this miracle all depends on you. The first step to accepting this miracle all depends on you.

You have to unlock your own mental door. Your own hand is on the doorknob all you have to do is twist the door open. Once you do that, the ideas will flow right in. You're asking yourself, "John, how the heck do I do that? Simple. Stop having expectations! We create so many mental barriers based on what we hear, see, taste, and feel.

Stop it! Do everything as if you have no expectations and let things just happen. Allow your mind to expand past your own perceptions. If someone asks you to dance (you don't like dancing only because you think you suck at it . . . well, too bad!), get down and start doing the worm!

When you open your mind, you become an awesome person and, more importantly, you begin to get great ideas. For those who already have a great idea, when you open (perhaps "re-open") your mind you begin to further develop your idea.

> Creativity is just connecting things. When you ask creative people how they did something, they feel a little guilty because they didn't really do it, they just saw something. It seemed obvious to them after a while.
> —Steve Jobs

Albert Einstein has many encouraging messages relevant to entrepreneurs. I'm going to paraphrase a few of those concepts here:

Intellectuals solve problems; geniuses prevent them. It is a miracle that curiosity survives formal education. Things should be made as simple as possible but not any simpler. Strive not to be successful but rather to be of value.

Now that you're in a good mood, let's further develop your idea by putting it on paper.

Exercise Four: Put Your Idea to Paper

1. Below, write down your idea using one sentence and no more than one comma.

_____

_____

_____

_____

2. Some ideas are complex, but if the average Joe doesn't understand it and/or doesn't see value in it, you better have a lot of money backing you up. If you do not, then you need to stare at the sentence from step 1 and re-write it until it makes more sense. Rewrite your idea here.

_____

_____

_____

_____

_____

_____

Here is an example of how it might look:

1. My XYZ Company is developing a social, web-based seating check-in platform to help air travelers see who is on their flight and use Facebook and LinkedIn to assign all flight seats with one click.

2. The above description lets me know clearly what the company does, how they are going to do it, who they target, how they target, and it sounds great. You will lose your audience's attention if you take more than a few sentences, so put some effort and time into the description, ensuring it's a single, informative sentence.

3. Rewrite your sentence using the above sample as a template (this is a critical step before moving on to the next miracle)._____

_____

_____

_____

To read more real one-sentence pitches and share yours as well, please visit my Facebook page:

facebook.com/entrepreneurshiptherawtruth

Develop the Idea

Receiving the workable idea is a miracle, but that's only the first step. Developing the idea with the proper team is the most important step. In order to receive the second miracle—the proper teammates—your idea has to be developed into a full-fledged vision. That vision is represented in the one-sentence pitch. The better the pitch the stronger the hook you have to attract, retain, and support your vision.

If you haven't poked holes in your idea (looking at it from every angle, discerning all the possible shortcomings, etc.), someone else will. At this stage, you should be able to answer questions about the idea. If you can't answer a question, then it's time to make a careful and critical examination of the idea.

Most importantly, don't be the one who tells someone an idea and then fails to answer the first question you get. In order to receive the second miracle, you must do everything in your power to know more than anyone else about your idea!Most importantly, don't be the one who tells someone an idea and then fails to answer the first question you get. In order to receive the second miracle, you must do everything in your power to know more

than anyone else about your idea!

Second Miracle: The Team

Steps to Building a Team

You will know you have received the second miracle when you have attracted and built a team that can operate without you holding their feet to the fire. However, the first step to allowing this miracle to occur has nothing to do with building a team!

The very first thing you need to do is (reality) check yourself. Quickly go back over the entrepreneurship chapter. Remember, you set the standard. If you're weak, the team will be weak. If you're strong, the team will be strong.

This step is very difficult. I am going to ask you to do something hard. You *will not* succeed if you do not get rid of bad friends or negative influences you have in your life. I am fully aware I sound like your mom or dad, but let me explain.

We all have that one friend that only calls when they need something, is a little too wild at parties, always guilt trips us about everything, and so on. You don't invite them to family events because they

> **Comment [7]:** It seemed repetitive in light of "too wild at parties" but if these phrases have different meanings, please reject the deletion.

might embarrass you. You know who they are. They might be a brother, sister, friend, girlfriend, etc. You will not receive the second miracle if you don't get rid of them.

These "friends" are not bad only for you; they repel good people you might be trying to attract. Those who come across your toxic "friends" and don't know them will *not* put up with their nonsense. Trust me when I tell you...tell me who your friends are and I'll tell you who you are.

For those of you who have a negative significant other, run away! It's time to get rid of that baggage. You're an entrepreneurial person, a visionary. How can you say you're a visionary yet you can't see twenty years down the road with your significant other who is going to nag you and question your every move? Again, I don't mean to sound like your parent, but the number one reason entrepreneurs fail is because of this exact reason. Think deep, think hard, and do what needs to get done.

Ask any investor, mentor, or smart businessman, and they will all tell you that teams are what make things happen, no matter what the idea is. It's not just the corporate teams, but your everyday-life teams—spouse, children, friends, and family. I really hope you have the strength to do this. The next exercise is the first step you need to take.

Exercise Five: Weed Out Negative Influence

Write down the names of ten of your friends. Remember, "Let Go" does not mean you'll never interact with these people again; it just means that you're going to give yourself space from them for the time being, in the greater interest of achieving your goals.

1. _____ Keep / Let Go
2. _____ Keep / Let Go
3. _____ Keep / Let Go
4. _____ Keep / Let Go

5. _____ Keep / Let Go

6. _____ Keep / Let Go

7. _____ Keep / Let Go

8. _____ Keep / Let Go

9. _____ Keep / Let Go

10. _____ Keep / Let Go

Be proud of yourself. I know how hard this is. For the ones that you circled "Let Go," what you need to do next is call, text, or e-mail them, and let them know you will be very busy for the next few months. Trust me when I say they won't even reply or call, they will just keep doing what they have been doing, which is to call you when they need something. At that point all you have to do is ignore them.

You might be asking yourself, "Why am I doing this?" This concept is one of the hardest to accept due to the emotional connection we think we have with particular individuals. This concept applies to both our personal and professional lives. It's amazing how even the most seemingly innocent, infrequent interactions can impact us. We need to seek out people who help us, not drown us.

Prep for the Team

Before you even start thinking about getting other people onboard, you need to do as much work as you can. If you are starting a tech company and you are not technical, you can still do a lot of work without getting a technical partner right away.

Based on your idea, you might be limited to how much you can do alone. Chances are you can test your idea's fundamental purpose on your own. Let's say you want to open up a smoothie store but you don't know if people will like it. You can visit your local farmers' market website, pay to reserve a spot, get all the necessary equipment and branding, and then test your product in the "real world." Ah, it's much easier said than done, but possible.

This same concept applies to many industries. If you are in the tech industry, you can apply this concept by building mock-up apps using POP in the Apple app store. My point is: if you really are an entrepreneurial person, this is where you show it. You have to do whatever it takes to get as much work done on your own before you consider bringing in people. If you can't get hold of a free way of testing your idea, then you are going to have to spend money developing it to attract a specific partner. If you are a technical entrepreneur, don't look for a business-minded partner; look for someone who can help you distribute your idea at a fixed cost *and* be a mentor who can help you negotiate like a shark.

When to Look for a Partner

When you need help getting to the next phase of your development, or need help in the areas that you are not an expert in—e.g., distribution channels, HR, legal, fundraising, technical, etc.—then it's time to bring in another person (or people).

It's important to make a distinction between partners and employees. If the workload becomes overwhelming simply because you have too many orders and not enough people to fill them, what you need is an employee, not a partner.

Looking for a partner is like being a lead singer looking for a drummer. Your partner has to be someone who plays an instrument you can't play, is in sync with your vision, and has the same discipline you have to reach that vision.

OK, fine, you really want to know how to get a partner, or "teammate." Here we go!

> **Comment [8]:** This is a nice analogy that almost everyone can understand and that perfectly describes the fit between partners.

> **Comment [9]:** I think this paragraph would flow much better after the Beatles quote to start the next chapter. That way, the direct address to the reader will really play well when people skip right to that chapter.

> My model of business is the Beatles. They were four very talented guys who kept each other's negative tendencies in check; they balanced each other. And the total was greater than the sum of the parts.... Great things in business are never done by one person; they're done by a team of people.
> —Steve Jobs (2003)

Attract and Retain Talent

In the previous chapter, we discussed how to turn your idea into a vision. We did this by creating your one-sentence pitch. This pitch is the hook you need to land the right fish. Entrepreneurial people don't just fish anywhere; they find the perfect spot out of the entire ocean of people. Once you find your spots to fish, you can begin to hook people. If you truly are an entrepreneur, you won't just have a great pitch; you'll also deliver it in a charismatic and epic way.

> "Do you want to spend the rest of your life selling sugared water or do you want a chance to change the world?"
> —Pitch by Steve Jobs to John Sculley to join Apple, 1985

Comment [12]: Might need to check some of the dates attributed to these quotes. Sculley's Wikipedia article says he became CEO at Apple in 1983, so that suggests this quote is likely from before 1985. The same article also quotes Jobs differently than here.
http://en.wikipedia.org/wiki/John_Sculley#1983.E2.80.9393:_Apple_Inc

With a great vision and with all your homework done, you will have the tools you need to attract great people within your network. Remember, it doesn't matter how big or amazing your idea is; no one will (nor should) work for free. When you really need people, give them what they're worth—and don't be greedy. Note: 100 percent of zero is zero, but 30 percent of a million dollars is three hundred thousand dollars that you didn't have before. Be smart; get advice. For example, you could reserve 25 percent of all company stock for future valuable employees, venture capitalists, angels, etc., and then split the remaining 75 percent with yourself and other key team partners.

Finally, don't make any major decision without first consulting your mentors or advisors. At the very least, go online and research nonprofit organizations like SCORE.org and get a mentor. The second miracle will not take place if you don't take your time and make the right decision.

> You want to be extra rigorous about making the best possible thing you can. Find everything that's wrong with it and fix it. Seek negative feedback, particularly from friends.
>
> —Elon Musk

Third Miracle: Window of Opportunity

The Miracle Explained

The third miracle is simple. It's when the market notices you and gives you a chance to prove your product or service. The first time I experienced this miracle, I cried. This will be a huge moment for you, the moment you've been waiting for.

I cried because of the struggles, challenges, disappointments, and frustrations that not only I had to go through, but also those my team had to go through. This was a bittersweet moment. As the cofounder and CEO, it was my job to keep everyone motivated, on task, and focused on the vision. My team and I had been working around the clock; we scarified holidays, family time, money, other opportunities, relationships, etc., all in order to keep going, without any guarantees of success.

To give you a real-life example, after a month of preparing we had finally developed and trained a sales team to go out and canvas the area. The first day we went out, I took one guy with me and we visited twenty-six locations from 8 a.m. to 8 p.m. We signed up five locations that day, which was an awesome day for the both of us. However, afterward I went back to the office and had to digitize all the contracts. I didn't leave the office till about midnight, knowing that I was going to do it all over again the following day with another teammate. I had this routine for a whole summer; at first our conversion rate was less than 10 percent. By the end of the summer, with more practice and experience, we signed over three hundred locations with a 30 percent conversion rate.

For those of you who will be lucky enough to experience this miracle, be careful. In my experience it tends to want to drag you through the mud before it presents itself to you. I was ready to give up and shut the doors of my company when out of nowhere we began to close deals left and right. We then began networking and attending conferences to present ourselves to investors whom we specifically targeted. We began to look for funding, and within three months we closed our first deal. We got enough capital to finally stop eating Top Ramen every other day.

On my laptop I have a quote that says, "Remember the guy who gave up? Neither does anyone else." The secret is to not give up; instead, ask for advice, seek help, and keep going. This miracle is famous for pushing you to the edge before it fulfills itself; that's why I call it the "rare and tricky miracle."

If something is important enough, even if the odds are against you, you should still do it.

—Elon Musk

Timing

Timing. What a concept. It's the one thing none of us fully understands—especially entrepreneurial people. We as visionaries see things most people don't, but we also don't have a clear idea when others will begin to see what we see. Visionaries like us can clearly see the future; the stronger we see it the more passionate we are about creating it. If I am not making sense to you, let me better explain with this amazing example.

In 1987, Apple released a product video of a professor using what looks a lot like the iPad. Over twenty-six years ago, Steve Jobs had a solid vision of what the iPad would look like and how it would function. Jobs's ability to see the future of human interaction with technology was spot on, but the timing was off. The technology was not there; and if it had been it would have been way too expensive for the average consumer. The beauty is that this didn't stop Steve Jobs from realizing his dream of a screen in your hands that could be controlled with your finger motions and voice. For twenty years, Jobs and his team worked on what we now call the iPad; in other words, Jobs and his team prepared the iPad idea for twenty years, waiting for the world to be ready for the product (i.e., to need the product). Apple released the iPad in early

2010. In the first year, the iPad made over one hundred million dollars in revenue.

Being overly prepared for any opportunity that might present itself is the key to receiving this miracle. Preparing for something as simple as a test or job interview to something as complex as a service or product that will revolutionize the way we interact with technology makes no difference. It all starts with how hard you are willing to prepare for an opportunity that may present itself in the future.

> We're gambling on our vision, and we would rather do that than make "me too" products. Let some other companies do that. For us, it's always the next dream.
> —Steve Jobs, January 24, 1984

There are so many amazing entrepreneurial people I could talk about, but Jobs is by far the pinnacle of entrepreneurship in our recent history. Timing is such an insane concept, yet one man was able to harness it a little bit, and that was Steve Jobs. Jobs's ability to see the future was so intense that he essentially had his own reality. Many people thought Jobs was crazy because they clearly could see he believed his own reality and not everyone else's. This is something entrepreneurial people struggle with, and maybe this is why Jobs didn't take his cancer so seriously in the beginning.

There was one thing Jobs had been working hard to realize in his lifetime that he didn't see come to fruition; unfortunately, his life ended before he could receive the miracle. In the summer of 2009, Jobs contacted Foster and Associates to design a new headquarters for Apple's thirteen

> Comment [15]: Which miracle?

thousand employees. Jobs recognized that where we work is very important to our productivity, our well-being, and, most importantly, our creativity. Jobs understood this more than any one of us. Being a great entrepreneurial leader, he knew the three main aspects of a great organization: culture, talented people, and an amazing and inspiring workplace for these people. This trifecta motivates and inspires innovation. Jobs had already done a great job building a culture and attracting the best people to Apple. The last thing he wanted to accomplish was to see the working space that would facilitate further inspiration and growth at Apple. Jobs ran out of the one thing that is most precious to all of us, time.

The Apple headquarters is expected to be completed in 2015. It will be over 2.3 million square feet and house thirteen thousand employees. It will be considered a modern-day marvel, just like Steve Jobs. The lesson is: we all get opportunities. Are you prepared for the opportunity to be extraordinary?

> We don't get a chance to do that many things, and everyone should be really excellent. Because this is our life. Life is brief, and then you die, you know? And we've all chosen to do this with our lives. So it better be damn good. It better be worth it.
> —Steve Jobs

> **Comment [16]:** Slightly different quote here: http://money.cnn.com/galleries/2008/fortune/0803/gallery.jobsqna.fortune/4.html

Exercise Six: Describe the Experience

Do yourself a favor and write down how you felt and what it cost you to receive this miracle. I left you a whole page to do so. Then share your thoughts with others! Let them know it's possible!

Fourth Miracle: Live or Die

The third miracle sets you up for the hardest phase of your life, the final miracle. The miracle I call, "Live or Die." Most entrepreneurial people don't survive this miracle due to how unprepared or overwhelmed they get. This miracle will truly test you as a person, and if you receive it—you've made it.

Respect the Success

You know you're successful when you go from one thousand customers, users, or fans, to one million. So many of us want to receive this miracle, yet so many of us are not prepared for it. This is why most of us who reach this point fail. It isn't because we don't want it, it's because we likely didn't plan big enough, didn't build the infrastructure, and perhaps because we personally weren't ready to sacrifice everything for it.

You have to give up everything in order to gain everything. Those who give up their weekends or work over eighty hours per week, etc., are the ones who succeed. I know this might seem hard at first, but it's only temporary. It takes time to put the proper system in place, but once you do, your workload will decrease dramatically.

Be Honest: Recognize Epic Failures

Let me give you a great example of an organization that experienced three of the four miracles. This organization is going to

> **Comment [17]:** Does "organization" refer to the Obama administration, or just Obamacare? I think the "epic fail" specifically refers to Obamacare, but I wouldn't call that an organization. Also, is the epic fail really just the website roll-out, or is it all of Obamacare? From what follows in the manuscript, it seems like you're saying Obamacare as an idea is fine (thus not the epic fail), and that Healthcare.gov was the real failure. It's unclear where the failure is being attributed.

go down as one of the biggest unnecessary "epic fails" of our time. Yes, I am talking about Obamacare. All political persuasion aside, the Obamacare website thus far has been such an epic failure in so many respects that it would be insane for me not to use it as the greatest example of a team failing to receive the fourth miracle. What follows is how the evolution of this failure may have looked.

An entrepreneurial person had an idea to provide more people with affordable healthcare. Hey, it's a great idea. Who doesn't want healthcare that's affordable? I give this person an insane amount of credit for having such a big and challenging idea. Like I mentioned in the entrepreneurial idea chapter, the bigger the idea the better (first miracle).

In this specific case, the second miracle only comes into play for the most part after the epic failure of the idea (on October 1, 2013), when many famous industry-leading tech wizards decided to help out with Healthcare.gov. The reason the second miracle applies is because these amazingly talented people would not have decided to help if they didn't believe in the vision and perceived value it's supposed to have for the average American (second miracle).

As the leader, your job is to live and breathe the vision by sharing it with everyone you meet. Obama did just that with affordable healthcare. He began to travel the country and promote his vision by repeating a few key words: "affordable healthcare for all." He was able to get the market excited about his product with the help of every major media outlet, celebrity endorsements, PR campaigns, etc. Don't get me wrong—he did an amazing job getting the word out. He worked very hard to let the market know what he was doing, harder than most entrepreneurs I know (and the people I know work really hard.) Almost everyone was anxious to taste his product (third miracle). On October 1, 2013, his product was released to the public, users rushed to taste it, and all they got was a punch in the mouth.

Like I mentioned above, you never get truly tested until you reach the footsteps of the fourth miracle. Obamacare's execution failed! At this point we can't point fingers; instead, we need to see how we can quickly correct the reason we didn't receive the fourth miracle. More often than not, we burned through all our capital and missed our chance. In this case, with endless amounts of capital (our tax dollars), the president can keep trying to buy his fourth miracle. He will receive the miracle only if he can deliver the goods. If not, he never will—not even with all the money in the world.

> **Comprehensive Copy E..., 5/2/14 2:20 AM**
> **Comment [18]:** Why is "we" being used? Isn't Obamacare the subject of the example? If the discussion is going back to focusing on the reader, there needs to be something to signal the transition from Obamacare. As it reads now, it seems like you are saying we can't point fingers at people in the Obama administration, but I don't think that's what you're trying to say.

Yes, I know, you can't believe that even with all of the president's resources he still failed. The raw truth is that for most of us, whatever we do, since we don't have the same resources or endless amount of start-up capital, our chances of success are much lower. Even a great idea—with the best team, start-up capital, and market viability—could fail. I'm not saying this to discourage you, only to let you know that no miracle I mention in this book is a guarantee, especially the fourth.

For most of you, you are still waiting to reach this miracle, if not the third miracle. At the current moment, I haven't received the fourth miracle myself. However, if you are reading this book, it may have been placed on *The New York Times* Best Seller list, and in that case I have received this miracle.

Receiving these miracles is not easy, but I know for a fact you won't receive even one of them unless you try. Greatness is for those who try, those whose entrepreneurial spirit burns strong, those who are visionaries, those who are pioneers, those who have endless commitment, and those who are willing to risk it all, fail, and do it all over again.

Doesn't End Here

Congratulations! You made it to the last chapter of this book. Unlike many entrepreneurial wannabes, you are the real deal. You finish what you start.

Just to be clear, the fourth miracle is not the last one. I wrote this book to show you how to be successful and, most importantly, to reveal the simple yet always overlooked secret ingredient—timing!

> **Comprehensive Copy E..., 5/5/14 2:16 AM**
> **Comment [19]:** This first paragraph will really make the readers feel good about their progress.

You can't buy a miracle. Obama couldn't do it with billions of dollars and neither can you. The miracles can only be received at their own time. Now that you know this, you can see things for what they truly are. No one holds the magical secret for you but yourself. Only you can decide to pursue your dream, only you can stay committed to your dream, and only you have the power to stay faithful and true to yourself—especially when the world tries to manipulate you to do otherwise.

I don't have all the answers and neither do other people. Even if I did have all the answers and told them to you, you would have to be ready to receive them in order to truly hear and understand them. What I want you to do is use your critical thinking skills. Take the information I provided in this book and analyze your own surroundings, your own networks of people, resources, etc.

It's time for you to wake up to your own reality. Not the reality of others on Facebook, Twitter, Instagram, etc. Turn off those distractions, and get inside what I call your own "Superman Fortress of Solitude." It's that place where you can actually hear yourself and focus on your own thoughts. I have a few of these fortresses: behind the wheel, on the toilet, and in the shower. So, do yourself a favor…GET TO WORK! Hope you enjoyed the information.

Thanks again for reading this book, I really appreciate it. Wish you the best, your friend, John D. Monjazi.

Dedication

For those of you who don't know me, my name is John D. Monjazi. I am an entrepreneurial-minded person who has built, sold, failed, and, most importantly, learned from every venture I've been involved with since I was sixteen years old.

In 2013, I went to a summer camp as a chaperon for high school kids, located at Palomar Mountain, California. It was great—a whole week in the mountains, three meals a day, and completely disconnected from the world. I was amply able to focus on my life and getting to know the kids.

Every night at about 10 p.m., once all the boys were drained of their energy, we would all meet in the middle of the building to talk and get to know each other. Every night we would get deeper and deeper. By Thursday night the boys and a few chaperons began to talk about the deep pains and struggles they faced. By Friday night, most of the boys had cried after they had openly talked about the deep hurt they experienced while growing up. What

> **Comment [20]:** Was this a cabin? What kind of building was it? A reader needs to get some kind of description to form a basic image of the setting.

shocked me to my core was that every single one of those kids and chaperons all had one thing in common: their deepest pains and hurts all originated from the same place, their parents.

There were two twin boys, both of them very deeply hurt due to their father's abandonment and their mother's consistent trips in and out of jail due to drug addiction. Shockingly, every one of the kids who shared had an impactful story of how they lacked confidence, self-esteem, goals, motivation, hope, security, etc., because they did not have a mom or dad who cared for them, loved them, or was there for them.

This book would not have been possible if it were not for my mom and dad, whom I consider my heroes. I realize my dad is my biggest fan and my mom is my biggest cheerleader. I cannot thank them enough for everything they have taught me, the way they raised me, the way they disciplined me, and most importantly all the love they have demonstrated.

Mom, Dad, I love you guys so much. Thank you for bringing me into this world and taking care of me. So many people do not get to experience what I did, and I am eternally grateful for the both of you.

Love you,
John D. Monjazi

www.ingramcontent.com/pod-product-compliance
Lightning Source LLC
Chambersburg PA
CBHW020925180526
45163CB00007B/2891